The TENACITY To Do It Anyway

copyright © 2011

Tenacity - Making Your Dreams a Reality

PHYLLIS L. JONES

iUniverse, Inc.
Bloomington

The Tenacity to Do It Anyway
Tenacity - Making Your Dreams a Reality

All Scripture used in this document are taken from the King James Translation (public domain) of the bible. FYI this translation was requested to be done by King James VI in 1604. This translation now used in the United States was done by 47 scholars from the Church of England and completed by them in 1611. There are many translations of the bible; they are just tools useful in helping build a relationship between an all mighty God and all of mankind which He created and which He loves.

iUniverse books may be ordered through booksellers or by contacting:

iUniverse
1663 Liberty Drive
Bloomington, IN 47403
www.iuniverse.com
1-800-Authors (1-800-288-4677)

Because of the dynamic nature of the Internet, any web addresses or links contained in this book may have changed since publication and may no longer be valid. The views expressed in this work are solely those of the author and do not necessarily reflect the views of the publisher, and the publisher hereby disclaims any responsibility for them.

Any people depicted in stock imagery provided by Thinkstock are models, and such images are being used for illustrative purposes only.
Certain stock imagery © Thinkstock.

ISBN: 978-1-4759-4435-8 (sc)
ISBN: 978-1-4759-4436-5 (ebk)

Printed in the United States of America

iUniverse rev. date: 08/27/2012

CONTENTS

PART ONE
Tenacity—Who It Is and Who It Is Not

PART TWO
Tenacity—My Stories

DEDICATION

This is dedicated to the One I love. He chased me for a long time before I realized I needed Him. We have only been close for twenty-one years but I have known about Him all of my life. I didn't think I was good enough to be close to Him; surely not in a relationship with Him, but my, my, was I wrong. I wasted a lot of time trying to ignore Him but He was so patient and waited for me to get over myself. One day I don't know what hit me but I fell so in love with Him and there are no words to explain it. My whole life has changed and I have indescribable joy.

This is dedicated to the One I love. He is always with me and I don't mind. If I feel like He is not near I get uneasy. He is a great listener and His wisdom is the best in this world. He is the only one who can always tell me what to do. No, I don't always listen but I quickly recognize when I should have listened, so I stop to ask Him for forgiveness and clear direction.

This is dedicated to the One I love. Just when I think I know Him; He keeps on surprising me. The way He answers me when I ask a question; sometimes His answer makes me wish I had not asked! You see His answers always require me to make a change and the change is always right. He loved me even when I was unlovable and just a total hot mess. He took the time to teach me how to live my life with joy. Nothing can separate me from Him and I never have to worry about Him leaving me because He has never broken any promises He has made to me. He is the best thing that ever happened to me.

This is dedicated to the One I love and I will love Him because He first loved me. The time limit on this love; He promised me eternity and since He holds time in His hand, our love will never end. Yes this one is dedicated to the One I love.

INTRODUCTION

TENACITY
Determination, diligence, persistence,
strength of purpose, strength of character

I have no clue where or when I first heard a voice telling me I needed to be more tenacious about the things in my life which have been identified as my passions. You know the things that are not a bucket list or a do before I die list, but the things that are a part of what and why I have life here on earth. I will not speak for anyone else, but for me I would always ask the question, why was I born? That question always came up when I was going through a tough time and wondered, what was the use; there has to be more to life than this! These times make me thankful only because I learn to appreciate the small things in my life and they invoke my imagination to begin to dream of the things that my heart desired.

I love to think about a child who usually around the age of four or five, begins to ask why and for every answer you give them they come back with another why. I have come to understand that one of the characteristic of a tenacious person is that they never, ever accept a no, you just can't do it, or it is not possible, as the answer to their why question. They will always ask why not; why can't I write a book, design dresses, build a house, start a day care, and go back to school. The cemetery is full of people who never realized their passion while they were here on earth usually because they looked at the passion as being dreams deferred and even allow their own doubts to stop them from living out the dream.

There is a place in the world that only I can fill and it was designed especially for me. No one else can fill that place, that purpose, that connection to others, but me. Beloved, it is the same thing for you. I am born to encourage others not to give up. To believe that you can do anything you put your mind to if you believe you can do it. Your journey may not follow the way that others have gone but there is a way already prepared for you to go, so you should not give up on the dream.

Wouldn't you know that this book became a great teacher of how to be tenacious in believing it can be done and an even better teacher in learning not to procrastinate or put off moving towards the end goal. It is a short book and no doubt if you could count the many times I told everyone I was writing a book until now, they are expecting a five hundred page novel but sometimes good things come in small packages.

Phyllis L. Jones

ACKNOWLEDGMENTS

There are treasures in earthly vessels and I would like to acknowledge the treasured vessels that have been assigned to me. My children, Derrick and Shelby and my granddaughter, Jade. My step sons and daughter, Elwood, Anthony and Michele' and my little grandsons, Micah and Mikhale, along with the rest of my family, friends and church family, I love you all.

Alfreada Brown-Kelly for sharing her book writing experiences with me and Donna, Herbert and Reverend Stovall for your creative insights towards my goal. To Grace, Mary, Janet and Rev. Chris for your encouragement to finish it already; I love you all.

Thank you Reverend Dr. Dwight Riddick, my pastor, your wife, my friend, Lady Vera. Together you have inquired from God on my behalf for so many years and today I get to tell you "thank you."

I also want to acknowledge the memory of James and Leola Montgomery, for adopting me and the memory of my husband James Jones for sixteen years of marriage before he went to be with our Lord. They are treasured vessels that brought me joy for a season.

My greatest words of gratitude go to a true and living God who walks with me every day. My protection, my way, my light, my help, my covering and my keeper; someone reading this knows what I mean, but if you don't I pray you do come to know Him for yourself. There is nobody like Him and I must say to Him "Thank You."

Finally to those who honor me by reading these pages, remember to love God, love yourself and love others; may you always be surrounded by God's love.

Phyllis L. Jones

PART ONE

Tenacity—Who It Is and Who It Is Not

Tenacity—Who It Is and Who It Is Not

IT IS . . . . Determined—Diligent—Persistence—Confident—Faith Filled

IT IS NOT . . . . Self Doubting—Full of Excuses—Fearful—Negative

Tenacious people are wise in that they realize they are responsible for creating the life they want to live. They set goals, dream dreams, have visions and look for ways to re-create themselves. They are willing to do what it takes to be a success in their career and in their personal endeavors. They also know that life will sometimes offer setbacks and problems along the way but they remain positive and press their way towards their goals. They realize that they are stronger than they thought they were and that the setbacks, enhances their character. Truth of the matter is it is seldom easy to get to the goal but the reward of accomplishing it is phenomenal.

Hebrews 11:1 (KJV) Now faith is the substance of things hoped for, the evidence of things not seen. The word **faith** as a noun means belief that is **NOT** based on proof. The word **substance** as a noun means; that of which a thing consists; physical matter or material form and substance. Now on the other hand the word **evidence** as a verb means; to make evident or clear, show clearly; manifest.

When we put this all together a tenacious person, who believes in a dream without having any proof, would not give up until the evidence of the dream is clear, manifested and available for all to see. Faith is an action word. It means we have to first believe in what we cannot see in the natural yet act as though it is real right now. Someone made the statement that we usually tell ourselves a story in our mind when we face a cross-road in our life. The story we tell ourselves will help us identify any negative thoughts that separate us from the dream.

There may be thoughts of fear. "I want to start that business but the economy is so bad right now it would be really foolish for me to think I could even begin to start it now. I need more capital and no one is going to give it to me. No one would want to even invest in my business and no banks are giving out loans." All of these statements could be true for someone who IS NOT tenacious. This person would not move forward after having proclaimed all these negative thoughts; they are defeated before they begin. Self doubt statements and lack of insight as to who they are fully able to become will always stand in their way.

A tenacious person will recognize that their way to accomplish this dream may be a route no one has ever taken before. They are dreamers of how to improve or create something outside of who they are. They are often referred to as those who walk to the beat of their own drum and they may even expect others to hear the same beat. No one in their family went to college, has a business, builds houses, write books or poetry, teaches, is a doctor or a lawyer but their dream is to be more than what they have become thus far.

I am totally convinced that the words "I Believe" are huge in their vocabulary, which brings it all back to having faith that God has placed more in them than they or anyone else may realize. That is why they can't listen to family or friends who are always set on telling them what they are not qualified to do. Their dream/vision causes them "to do it anyway" no matter what the obstacle is before them, they DON'T GIVE UP.

I have often read the above Hebrews 11:1 passage of scripture and as I have so often done, read right over something that has a deeper meaning. This is why the bible is the most wonderful book ever written and will always reveal new things to us each time we read it. The very first word in that scripture, in the King James translation, is the word "NOW." The faith that we exercise right now at this very moment of challenge or decision or lack of physical evidence, will produce the substance of the things we yet hope for. In other words if we have the faith to believe what we do not see right now the substance of our belief will materialize in the future. It means there is hope. This hope will also show up even bigger and better than what NOW faith can imagine it to look like. It does not always come from where we expect it to and it does not always look the way we think it will look but it comes in the biggest and best way possible for God to send into the world what His will is on earth; yes through you and through me, He is working out a plan.

Beloved I believe we are all sent with a purpose, a calling, with a meaning to this life we live. The problem with us is sometimes we don't think that our God given gift or talent is of value to anyone. What a great insult to our God, the creator of life. I really would love to break this down but I will save that for the next book, blog, online chat I will have with some of you. Let me just say that the tenacious person will always seek out the reason for things and seek to change things that need to be changed for the good of all. Why would anyone truly want to be born and die without knowing that their very presence on earth is a contribution to others? I have recently noticed a few commercials where a group of medical patients had the pleasure of meeting the employees who actually made their imaging testing machine and it was a beautiful sight to see the gratitude from the patients and the compassion and the pride of the employees; after all someone had to have the training to make the machine used to send images to doctors to help in their diagnosis of human illnesses. How often do we think of the person who came in to work and their job was to make something that we may take for granted yet we need to be healed? There is another commercial of a mechanic, who actually built the engines of trains which carry cargo across the country daily and when I sit at a railroad crossing I usually complain about how long I have to wait for this long train. No more complaining from me as I have a new appreciation for the work that went into that train moving all that merchandise from place to place and someone worked very hard to make it happen; benefit to you and me, cloths, shoes, food and many other items we use daily, thank you to all who made it happen. My point is often times the small things that seem unimportant to us, actually are very important. The person who cleans offices and public restrooms is very important. All people who work in a service capacity are important to us all yet often taken for granted. The tenacious service person may be someone who loves to clean and would seek to open their own home cleaning business and yes I would hire them to help me. This is a dream for them and a gift for others. Those who love to bake, cook, sew, draw, design are all gifts to others who may not have the gift, talent or desire to do any of the above things.

Truly the answer to the question of what our purpose is has to do with the things we may do every day and maybe we don't think of it as valuable, important or marketable to others. The things we do that we enjoy so much we forget to eat and we get involved doing for hours, even without pay. Oftentimes others will recognize our gifting before we do simply because we just think of it as something we do but not really that important.

Finally for those who feel like you have no purpose, vision, or dream, get one. Look for ways to give to someone who needs help. Become tenacious in the search for a higher purpose of service in your life. Remember our days here on earth are numbered and we don't know when the last day is so get busy now, make a difference now and don't put off for tomorrow what you can do today. The thing you may view as not important is very important to someone. All I am doing is calling you to a time of service to others. The reward for doing so is beyond anything you can imagine. I am saying to the person who is already tenacious; keep thinking out of the box. Even if you have already realized the dream kick it up a notch. We service a God who gives us desires and dreams and He is not one who can be put in a box. We often try to put Him in one when we use little faith and think that things are not possible even with His help. With God all things are possible as long as it is according to His will. His will is that we love each other and demonstrate this love by serving each other. I know I am right so just try it and see how wonderfully indescribable you will feel within. Seek God's wisdom in all things you do and believe me He is waiting for you to come to Him and ask for help; which He so willingly wants to give. We are the manifestation of God's love and presence on earth; it's in the plan. Jeremiah 29:11-13 [11] For I know the plans I have for you," declares the LORD, "plans to prosper you and not to harm you, plans to give you hope and a future. [12] Then you will call on me and come and pray to me, and I will listen to you. [13] You will seek me and find me when you seek me with all your heart. Enough said.

PART TWO

Tenacity—My Stories

GPS JOURNEYS

<u>G</u>od <u>P</u>lans <u>S</u>trategic Journeys in the life of men and women. Our destiny is in His hand and has already been mapped out before we were yet in our mother's womb. (Jeremiah 1:4, 5)

Every tear shed weather happy or sad, every pain and heartache, every smile and time of laughter is included in the journey. His directions are always right but there are times we decided we know the best way to go

RECALULATING

Just the same as being on a road trip when we take the route that we chose instead of the one programmed in our GPS system we hear, "recalculating," but then we are told to go left, go right, or make a U turn to get us to the desired destination. Likewise God's plan will get us to the desired destination and we can have eternal life with Him.

HONORING OUR FALLEN SOLDIERS

How do you say thank you to the fallen soldiers of war? They indeed made the ultimate sacrifice for us all. It was not given to them to debate whether the war they gave their life for was right or wrong, but rather that they went to protect the innocent and to promote freedom to all mankind, at home and abroad. They are fathers, mothers, daughters, sons, husbands, wives, sisters and brothers, serving in places where there is no guarantee of a tomorrow, yet they face every day with the knowledge that this may be their last day. It is so possible that being prepared to fight for the rights of others is their dream and they gave their life for that dream. These soldiers consider it to be an honor to serve others in this way. They prepare themselves to protect those they share their life with daily and to protect those they don't even know.

How do we say thank you to the fallen soldiers of war? First, we remember them in our prayers and remember the families they leave behind. These families have been changed forever. Honor them by helping to restore the soldiers who return home wounded in their physical bodies and also in their mental and emotional spirits. They need medical care to be restored and placed back into society where they can live meaningful, productive and fulfilling lives. Our fallen soldiers have fought right next to our wounded soldiers and they both deserve all we have to give to show our appreciation for their sacrifice.

They will never be forgotten and they live on in our hearts and memories. We are thankful that we can walk every day in the freedom for which they gave their lives for us.

SINGLE ACCORDING TO PLAN

I want to write this article according to what God has done in my life. I would imagine that along the way you may have had some of the same experiences and if you have not, just keep living. I was single, married, divorced, single, remarried and now widowed and it has all been in God's plan for my life.

Why would I say it is all according to His plan? Simply because He states it in His word according to Jeremiah 29:11-13, God actually has a plan for my life, and He will work that plan no matter what I choose in life, He knows my beginnings and the exact way I will go. He has an expected destination for me. Listen beloved, I only know the first time I read that scripture I was so relieved that my future was not totally up to me. That means I have to listen whenever it is decision making time in my life and I have to trust in Him. Even if I missed it, He still has a plan. I am also convinced that if He laid His plan out for me, it would blow my mind. I know I could not handle it. This means I have to trust that no matter where I am, He resides with me.

I have been a believer in Jesus Christ for all of nineteen years, and I like to compare my life to the Word of God. I always advise my friends and whoever God sends into my pathway, to look for an example of your life in the bible. Believe me some biblical person's life is related to circumstances happening in your life right now. Singles are so very free to be used of God. Read about Ruth and Esther, single ladies who made an impact, so important in the lives of others around them. Their lives were used according to God's plan. It is the same today. Single men and women are important in God's plan and can be satisfied and single or single and desiring a spiritual connection. No matter which one of those two states of singleness I may find myself in I have learned to be thankful that my God has a plan just for me. I believe singleness is exciting. "For with God nothing shall be impossible," according to Luke 1:37. I choose to remain focused on my spiritual assignment, which will make room for my personal desires and listen carefully to the voice of God, because without it I am simply following my own plan. I thank God for my entire journey because it has helped me to learn many valuable lessons. I am aware of His presence, I am never alone, I am made whole in Him and I am a gift to others. I will use my singleness to glorify the God who has the plan for me.

**THE WAY WILL NOT ALWAYS
BE CLEAR; REFOCUS AND DON'T GIVE UP.**

THE GIFT OF YOU

Psalm 139:13-15

For thou hast possessed my reins: thou hast covered me in my mother's womb. [14] I will praise thee; for I am fearfully and wonderfully made: marvelous are thy works; and that my soul knowest right well. [15] My substance was not hid from thee, when I was made in secret, and curiously wrought in the lowest parts of the earth. (KJV)

I read that we are made unique and different from one another, therefore I can't "do you" and "you can't do me." Yet we offer each other the gift of ourselves as we share our life experiences and challenges with one another to continue our walk through life until our life mission/purpose is fulfilled. So, therefore I just want to tell you that it is not an option that you can choose to stop, give up, or just walk away from the person you are created to be. You are needed to fulfill a specific purpose in life. Never allow anyone to makes you feel like you are not important to someone, somewhere.

Challenge yourself to do everything you have always dreamed of doing. The Gift of You to the world is your witness of a life lived through every obstacle and yet you are still standing. I will boldly say that there is no excuse not to be all you were created to be and the only reason it would not happen for you lies only within you.

There will always be some excuse that appears to stop you from fulfilling your destiny and you get to choose to not allow the excuses to weaken you.

Build your strength to continue by ignoring excuses and pushing pass blocked or closed doors.

THE SAME

Hebrews 13:8 - Jesus Christ the same yesterday, and today, and forever.

Same Lord, Same Peace, Same Joy, Same Mercy, Same Love, Same Help. Same Passion, Same Power, Same Strength, Same Light, Same Hope, Same Patience, Same Knowledge, Same Presence, Same Glory, Same Substance, Same Plan . . . . The Same

PINNED UP PRAISE

I am suffering with pinned up praise. Yes, pinned up praise needs a place to release. I woke up this morning and realized it was 7:00am. I am usually already in church, ready to worship God, in His house. I always wake up thanking Him for waking me up in the first place. Just have to say, "I love you," to Him. However this morning I did not say anything except, "Oh God I woke up late," and then I hopped out of bed and made my way to His house. Broke the speed limit and everything! I was so excited that I made it there until I realized that I had pinned up praise. I am telling you that pinned up praise can hurt you. It all begins to overflow out of you. The praise then turns to worship of Him and then it becomes so personal and so deep and intimate, just between you and Him and no one else.

Please don't get it twisted now. Pinned up praise can be released anywhere, not just in the four walls of the sanctuary, the church house, but also in your house, your car, your kitchen and it can be a small whisper, together with some tears, that make the connection between you and the Father.

A PLACE TO WEEP

How do you hide the pain that is growing on the inside, as you walk among people all day long? Pain that follows you everywhere you go. When you fall asleep at night, when you wake up in the morning, the same pain is still with you. There is more than one type of depression when you are dealing with deep pain. You deal with it by secluding yourself from others. You can also deal with it by appearing to be just fine as you go to work and interact with others but cry yourself to sleep each night. Sometimes this depressing pain will arise when you least expect it and you really want to just find a place to weep.

I believe the answer to this dilemma is found in the gift of time. In time the place in your heart will heal, and life will offer the opportunity to fill it with new love, new adventures, new people, and a new you. Soon you will start your life anew. That does not mean that your future life will not bring you to another need for a place to weep, but each time you do, you emerge stronger and wiser and confident, focused and competent to withstand trouble.

Be careful to watch for those around you, in your family or on your job who are looking for a place to weep. Encourage them and pray for them and be present for them. Don't be in such a big hurry with the things of life that you overlook them.

I have always found the place when I get silent, in the still small voice that whispers in my ear, "Come to me and I will give you rest and in my arms you will find a place to weep."

A LETTER TO JADE

Jade Nicole, Grandmother decided to drop you a line or two. Life, my darling, is a gift and how you decide to open the package is just as important as what is in it. At Christmas we open gifts and sometimes we take our time to remove each piece of tape so we can let the excitement of what we find inside build up inside of us. I like the above approach because when you open a gift quickly you may not like what's inside. The gift of life offers us many, many surprises, some good and some bad. You get to choose to keep what's on the inside or use the return policy. Then again life may send a non-return item, so you just have to deal with it.

I need to tell you, my dear child, you still get to choose how you deal with life. You can think a lot about it, stress over it and ring your hands or you can take the lemon, and make lemonade. All of life will be a series of choices, so remember to always do that which is right. How will you know what is right, you may ask me? The thing that is right will not bring sleepless nights to you. I did not say you may not have to choose that which is right and be hurt because of your choice. The choice will require you to leave some things and some people behind. If they are family, you may have to love them from afar. Always walk in dignity and love for others; know when to fight for right and when to just walk away. Choose your battles according to whether the fight will benefit an effective change to improve the life of many.

Phyllis L. Jones

I see within you many great things. Remember, to stay focused and stand tall. There is no one else, created by God, to fulfill your circle of life but you.

. . . . Grandma

NEVER

What time frame is that anyway? When is NEVER and how long does it last? How can you tell when it comes? How can you tell when it leaves? NEVER is not a time. It is what it is; it is NEVER!! I guess you can't be late for it, because it is NEVER. So how do you measure NEVER since it is what it is and it is NEVER? Sounds to me like a long time; NEVER, never comes.

Could it be the test of time when we declare it in our life? Peter told the Lord he would NEVER betray Him, but the Lord told Peter before the cock crows three times you will deny even knowing me. Peter's NEVER came sooner than he thought.

Be careful when you use the word NEVER. It can be a very long time or it can also be sooner than you think. Point taken!!

WRITE THE VISION, MAKE IT CLEAR.

TAKE A JOURNEY IN YOUR OWN LIFE?

Have you ever taken a journey in your own life? Well, I have and I'm back, and it was so worth the trip. All my bags are unpacked, and I see so clearly that it's not even funny. I see every friend, every enemy, every problem, with me and with others, every closed door, and every new open door.

Now that my reflections are finished with the past I will get on with my future. It is good to take the journey and dump all the baggage I should no longer be carrying.

LOVE EASY LIKE SUNDAY MORNING

The song says "Love won't let you wait," but sometimes love will make you wait. Why? Well, maybe He wants to see if you are ready for it or if you only think you are!! I mean do you know if you can even handle it when Love comes into your life? Sometimes Love would be easy like Sunday morning if you would just relax and let it do what it does. Sometimes Love will enter in and you run it away, never giving it a chance to (resonate) or flow and let go of all the boundaries you put up to keep Him out.

Love easy like Sunday morning, keeps you smiling when no one else is. Love easy like Sunday morning, sends you into a daytime day dream in the midnight hour. Love easy like Sunday morning lets you keep a song in your heart and a melody in your mouth. Love is easy, so easy, like a Sunday morning fills your heart with peace, joy and happiness. Love is easy, even when it is hard, so easy like Sunday morning!

Sunday is not the only day that Love shows up for you. Love is present Sunday through Saturday, yes 24/7 Love is present for you. Love will ask that you wait for that which is best for you, even when you think you know what is best. Love never forces Himself on you, but He will chase you down. Why, because He is Love and He desires to have a relationship with you.

He has penned 66 love letters to you so that you can see how much He loves you. You have always been on His mind from the very beginning of time. He gave birth to time when He said, "Let us create; it is done, it is finished, or it is eternal." Love is the Father of time and time is in His hand.

If you don't remember anything else, remember this, Love will make you wait when it is for your good. Love is easy like Sunday morning, so daily let Love in.

I DESERVE

I deserve to be happy, curl my toes into the sand
Stand in the rain, watch the water run through my hand

I deserve to be happy, watch the sun go down
As the stars come out and glitter all around

I deserve to be all God created me to be
I deserve to touch the lives of others so they can see

I deserve to create, I deserve to build
I deserve to empower and encourage according to His will

I deserve to love and to be loved in return
I deserve to dance, I deserve to sing
I deserve to soar like the eagle with my own wings.

THE GIFT OF TIME

I am so thankful for the many gifts that God gives to all of us. I try to stay focused on now, today, this minute, this hour and in so doing I become thankful to Him, because even in times when things aren't what I want them to be, my now, my present time, has GOOD in it. My now has me with a roof over my head, food to eat, clothes in my closet and shoes for my feet.

Many people in a city near me never imagined on Monday morning April 28, 2008 that everything they worked so hard for would be gone in a matter of a few minutes, all taken out by a tornado. Houses full of memories that they shared with their family are now gone, and life as it was just twenty-four hours earlier is no longer the same. Now what? I know this has been the question they have asked.

So, I think of the many things that I may daily take for granted because I expect them to be there. How many people do I take for granted because I expect them to be there? How many things do I put off for tomorrow because I expect tomorrow to come and I expect to be in it? **THE GIFT OF TIME** is from God. Tomorrow is not promised to us, only eternity with Him is promised to us. So, looking for things in my "now" to be thankful for is vitally important to me.

I want you to remember, for every child of God, there are many hidden talents. The loss of THINGS, yes, and people, will force the talents to appear in your life. There is the saying, "No pain, and no gain" and we know that we, like Jesus, all have a cross to bear as we go through life.

God, who knows everything, knows my timing for every minute of every day He allows me to wake up. God, who has the floor plan for my life, knows the things that are coming to me good and bad. God also knows what seems to be bad to me is yet working out for my good. Therefore, I try to remember these things I have come to know about my heavenly Father, and remembering helps me to embrace the scripture;

Matthew 6:25

[25]Therefore I say unto you, Take no thought for your life, what ye shall eat, or what ye shall drink; nor yet for your body, what ye shall put on. Is not the life more than meat, and the body than raiment?

S—T—R—E—T—C—H

Start Today Reaching Everything the Creator Has (For You)

Begin asking yourself if you have been listening to the spirit within you. There is more than you have **seen,** there is more than you have **done**; you are greater than you have **been**; you have more to offer to others than you have **offered**, there is more power within you than you have **released,** and there is more meaning to your life than you have experienced. You want your life to have meaning and purpose and so you have dreams and visions of what you think that purpose may be.

Start to give your thoughts permission to create the biggest dreams you have ever had for your life. What is stopping it from happening? What would it take to make it happen? Have you allowed yourself, to stop long enough to believe your dreams can be your reality?

You have the power to create your future and build a life of endless wonders. Since you are included in the original plans of God, there are times that He will S.T.R.E.T.C.H you. Now there is a difference between being stretched by God and being stretched by people. Let's examine closely which one you may be experiencing in your life.

To be stretched by people will suck all of your energy, time, money and mind, until you want to run away from home, work, and life. Only God is *all things* to *all people*. That's His job, not our job. (Psalm 121:4) 4Behold, he that keepeth Israel shall neither slumber nor sleep. So you need to turn off your mind and close your eyes and let Him work His Plan for your life. Never allow other people, yes and that includes your family sometimes, to suck you dry. Most of the stress and tension that we experience daily comes from being stressed by circumstances that sometimes are actually happening to others and not to us. We allow them to draw us into the drama of their lives. You can make a choice to not allow this to happen and still be at peace in your own life. Never let the choices of others steal the peace in your life. Ultimately, we have very little control over the choices that they make and even though we love them and would not want to see them suffer, IT IS THEIR CHOICE. To walk in the reality of your dreams will be more of an example of God's grace and favor to those you would want to make different choices in their lives, than anything you could say to them.

To be stretched by God will have you come out of your comfort zone and out of your box. You may start to feel uncomfortable on your job, in your relationships, and in your life in general. You may ask, "God is this going to be all there is to it for me? Is there more to life that I have missed according to the plan you have for me?" His answer would be "Yes, there is more to life, according to the plan I have for you." There are so many people who have lived and died but never lived His plan for them.

If God told you the whole plan, it would blow your mind, so God gives you little previews, and wouldn't you know it, some faint and some spend their whole lives running from just the previews. You have to stay focused, have faith and keep moving forward towards your goal. You can do it.

It is also true that you should never forget where you came from and that you need to remain humble in your character; you may need to change locations and the group of people you are around in order to move to the place God wants you to go. Be strategic in where you go and what you do and with whom you connect. Place yourself around those who are already doing what you want to do. They are gifts from God to lead you on your path. Remove all negativity, no matter if it comes from other people or from your own mind. Every "no, you can't" that comes your way, replace it with a "oh, yes, I can." Your coach (God) has the game plan all laid out, and He watches you play on the field of life and then brings you back into the locker room to draw out the next game plan until you have won the game. You need to look at the game plan to see the changes. If you don't see any changes, then maybe the plan did not need to change but you needed to change. You are as powerful as you allow yourself to be, simply because God has already given you what you need to make it happen. You are divinely made in His imagine, and you don't realize how powerful that is in and of itself. God never said it would be painless, but rather that the rewards would be great.

When you experience *every door* closing in your life, it is not always the enemy, but it could be God pushing you towards the plan He has for you. He is stretching you and asking you to look at the gifts, talents and dreams He has already given you, but you will not allow yourself to believe it can come true for you. Trust God, obey Him and go ahead and live your dream now. Don't give up, be patient, and don't allow negative thoughts or people to stop you from pursuing the dream which is already in you.

Remember that every failure is not always what it appears to be, but rather a closed door, indicating that you need to change directions because something better is waiting for you.

THE REASON I WEEP

I would say that life itself offers many reasons to weep. Life, being not always under my control, dictates many things to me that I truly did not ask to come my way, yet there are many things life brings that make me weep with joy. These joyful weeps I want to share because every time I think about them I still weep.

The birth of my son and my daughter and the first time I held them in my arms

I weep

The birth of my granddaughter with a cleft lip and three surgeries later, calling me "Grandma"

I weep

When I would watch my granddaughter and my husband play a game of checkers and accuse each other of cheating

I weep

When I go to church on Sundays after having one heck of a week, and I would hear Pastor Riddick preach words from God himself to me, I felt my soul respond with joy

I weep

When I hang out with my friends, my family and we are all present and laughing, playing games and acting silly, I go home at night alone, but I thank God for the time I shared with them

I weep

When my mind tries to remind me of all the things I do not have, my spirit speaks to remind me of all I do have. I have the ability to walk, to see, to talk, to hear, to speak and to dance. I have the ability to get wealth and bless others along the way. I have the freedom of self-expression in a world, where many do not have that privilege and many who do have it never use it. When I think of the life God has given me, so many more happy times than not happy times

I weep

When I weep, I weep with joy

CRAZY THINGS

Tell me why I keep reaching out to people

Who do crazy things and asking them to explain, to my satisfaction,

Why they did the crazy thing? O my mistake. It was a crazy thing

So why would I expect an explanation that would make sense to me?

I am not crazy so I would not understand. Lest I ask myself if the same event happened

To me, would I to do the same crazy thing? If the table turned would I think it not so crazy after all? Good question.

A FAMILY REUNION

This is an invitation to all our family to come to the family reunion.

Here is a list of things each person should bring:

*your sword and your shield

*an updated will

*olive oil

*black suit or black dress

*your sixty-six books (your bible)

*a chain and a hook (for binding the devil)

*a helmet

*a bell (to ring for time out during quarrels)

*a breast plate and knee pads

*flowers (in case you get laid out)

*urban dictionary (for translation between the generations)

*liquid soap (for mouth washing)

Get ready for a time to be remembered by all who will attend and talked about to those who do not attend.

I KNOW YOU

I know you
I know who you are
Why do you keep showing up in my life?

I know you
Same walk, same talk, same lies
We don't even have any soul ties,
Yet I know you

Every time you show up
As if it wasn't enough
My life always gets tough
Oh yes I know you

WEEPING SEED

What happens when the seed of Abraham weeps?

I have felt the pain of this recession in ways I have never experienced in my life before but I know giving up is not an option. Now I have heard that what does not break me will make me stronger. The question now is what happens when I have been beaten down to the ground?

I am from the seed of Abraham therefore when I feel the enemy has taken his foot to stump me into the ground I first recognize this is the best position he could have chosen for me to succeed. If you plant seed into the ground and water the seed it will break through the dirt and begin to grow a beautiful tree with much fruit.

Well I have cried some tears, not just for me but for many people all around me. I did not like my grounded position at first but I see a break in the soil, sunshine and light are coming through and this seed will rise and prosper.

My point is, no matter what has happened during these uncertain times I believe the best is yet to come. I have to wait for the sun to shine in my life again; and it will shine again. No recession or any other destruction can destroy the seed of Abraham.

MOMENTS OF GRATITUDE

Every day I wake up I experience sudden moments of gratitude.

Gratitude when I think about my family living and well.

Gratitude when I think about how will He use me today?

Gratitude when I think about a roof is still over my head and food in my house.

Gratitude when I think about my ability to move and think on my own.

Gratitude when I see the things I have prayed about the day before (like protection for me and my family) have carried over to the next day.

Yet I realize that it is God's plan that everything is as it should be accordance to that plan and I am not exempt from experiencing the loss and pain that others experience.

When there is a loss or pain in my life, my moments of gratitude increase in order to push out moments of discouragement as I walk by faith and not by sight.

My journey is but a brief moment in the larger plan God has for us, so it is of the utmost of importance that I take every opportunity to send up my moments of gratitude. Not just for what happens daily for Phyllis but also for what happens daily for others all around me.

Beloved, when it is all added up the rewards are so much bigger than any loss or pain we endure while we are here.

Join me in sending up moments of gratitude to our God all during each day. It will please Him and it will bring great thanksgiving, peace and joy to us.

DADDY AND ME

HOLDING HANDS IN THE PARK

I remember how I would feel when I went to the park with my daddy. He would always hold my hand and walk right beside me. He had this big bright smile on his face that I now know was his proud daddy look. As I looked up at him I saw the bright sunshine behind that big bright beautiful proud daddy smile. "This is my little girl," he would announce to his friends as we walked hand in hand.

I will never forget the day I had a fall on the steps at the park because I let go of his hand and ran ahead of him as he cautioned me to be careful. He rushed right to me and wiped my tears away and sat right down beside me with that same big smile and said "You are going to be ok; it is just a little scrape." "Let's go and get some Chocolate ice cream."

I remember it was at this time that he would just pick me up and carry me and I would lay my head on his strong shoulder as we went back to the car.

The other day I found this picture of a little chocolate girl holding her tall strong daddy's hand at the park. Those were the good old days and those are the feelings I will never forget.

When my daddy was 83 years old, I went to him as I was 41 years old and explained how excited I was to have given my life to Jesus Christ, September 8, 1991, as he was suffering a battle with cancer, unknown to me. During this time some people were afraid to be treated or cut on as they said for fear the disease would spread, but I remember seeing the same big smile on his face. November 12,

1991 he lost the battle and I lost the daddy whose shoulder I would lay my head or so I thought I had.

Much to my surprise, my daddy smiled because he knew I had given my life to the same one he himself had given his life to and that I would always have a hand to hold, a strong shoulder to lay my head, and yes someone to carry me when I fall.

AND HIS HAND GUIDES ME

WHAT I WISH YOU KNEW

What I wish you knew

How many times my pillow was wet with tears; how will I buy food and pay bills and keep a roof over your heads?

What I wish you knew

How many days I went to work sick but could not miss the time or pay

What I wish you knew

How proud I am of you when I see the strong, tenacious, independent, responsible person you have grown up to be

What I wish you knew

How much your grandmother loved you as she would always show up with a bag full of toys and she put up pictures of you as her eyesight was slowly fading away

What I wish you knew

I could never make those apple pies and yeast rolls your great-grandmother made for you before she died and I never took the time to write the recipe down

What I wish you knew

How I would cry on your first day of school and when you got your baby shot and when you left home to go out on your own

What I wish you knew

Being a single mom ain't easy but I had help all the time from above and I need you to know that if I had to do it all over again I WOULD

I Wish You Knew All That

MY LIFE, KOOL AID GOOD

I remember iced cold glasses of Kool Aid in basic cherry, orange, and grape flavors on a really hot summer day and yes usually there was always a request for a second glass. I remember growing up and preparing this same beverage for my two children and mixing the flavors together just to see what it would taste like. I really thought when all those other mixed flavors came out years later they got the idea from me, ha, ha. As I was just sitting around thinking, which I do a lot, I started to think about how my life was Kool Aid good.

Many different events make up the days of my life. They combine together to make my life Kool Aid good. Some events were bitter, others were oh so sweet but the mixing of those flavors makes me thankful for a good life. No matter what flavor you may be experiencing right now remember that the flavor today may be bitter and tomorrow may be sweet, but together they make your life Kool Aid Good.

SHORT AND SWEET

In spite of layers of impossibilities, one word from God will open up doors

Pray for deliverance from people and their opinions

Evolve into what you dream about and God will get the glory

Your life today can have peace which is better than granny's hot grits and butter

Dreamer, believer; which one are you?

A Seasonal Saint!! I'm so glad we don't serve a Seasonal God.

When you think of what you want to ask from God, you may be asking to small; think out of the box

When I ask God for wisdom I ask Him for Godly wisdom which far surpasses man's wisdom any day

Be a believer, not a doubter, be a doer, not just a viewer. When you see good get involved

From pain to peace comes from a relationship with God, not religion

Courage is just fear that has said its prayers

Move past your fear. Your reward is on the other side

Phyllis L. Jones

ENOUGH ALREADY

I am no longer surprised at what we read on all the social networks. My question would be the same to the youth or adult celebrities; why don't you take a moment to think and take a deep breath before you send out an often times emotional Twit or Facebook comment. I get excited when I think of all the millions of people we are able to connect with all over the world. There was a young woman who asked for anyone with type O blood to donate a kidney to her husband and she posted it on Facebook and they found someone. What a blessing the use of social media became in this case. It saved a life. I also shudder to think of the damage that can happen because of the emotional comments, some of which are demeaning to others that end up posted daily for everyone to see. There is way too much information released, much more than most of us want to know.

There are so many wonderful and helpful ways to help each other using these same social networks. People are able to quickly direct us to help with seeking jobs, getting necessary information for college preparation, health questions, words of encouragement, and a look into the life of people on the other side of the world. There are so many good things to share one with another but there are also times when we quickly respond to comments without thinking of who we may offend by our statement. I wish you would count to 100 before you type and allow your emotions to catch up with your comments. How many young people have committed suicide before they were made fun of in a huge public way? Sometimes no response speaks louder than anything we could think of to say.

There are some really excellent videos posted as well but then there are some that should remain private. Once you post these things out into the atmosphere there is no way to recall them back from the millions of eyes that view them. Listen I love to hear about certain people in politics or entertainers but some things about their life should remain private. Enough already and I don't want to know. I hear entertainment programs announce that they are about to show the store that some entertainer was seen shopping in today, guess what I don't care where they were shopping!!! If you show me the video of them helping the homeless or serving food to less fortunate people, this I want to see. The truth of the matter is many, many celebrities help people by giving of themselves, giving their money as well but it is not blown up as much as who they went out with last night. I don't care. Talk about their good and pray for them when they have troubles in their life. Show them compassion. What I know for sure is I am not alone in feeling that way. I am always excited when someone takes the time to report that a person, famous or not has done a kindness for someone else. This helps me to know that the entire world has not gone to hell in a hand basket; there are people who care for others and help others without expecting something in return. If it is helpful or good clean and hilarious humor I am all in but hurtful or harmful information count me out.

Remember my recommendation to count to 100 before you hit the keys and maybe no response is the right response to most comments; either way I just had to say Enough Already.

I KNOW WHO I AM

I know who I am and because you see me as someone else does not make it true. I remember working as a manager at a store and one of the customers was upset with me because he wanted to do something that was against our company policy so he proceeded to call me a B— at which point one of the female employees who passionately hates women being referred to by that name went pass me to confront the customer. I had to literally grab her to stop her and her question to me was "are you just going to let him walk away after calling you that?" Well my answer was yes, because I know who I am. I personally think that it made him look worse for saying it than it did for me to not respond.

My point for sharing this story is to tell some young person or maybe not so young person, to not waste your time, your energy or your dignity by responding to people who clearly do not know you. It is very hard to argue with someone when they are the only one speaking. Conversations happen between two people but yelling should be left up to the other person while you keep your blood pressure and stress levels down. I have often found that my silence will sometimes make a person angrier until they run out of steam and walk away. That is the very direction I would want to see them headed. There is also another option; I can just walk away.

I know who I am and I can stand up for myself. As a Kenny Rogers song says "You've Got to Know When to Hold em and

Know when to fold em, Know when to walk away and Know when to run." I will always show up as exactly who I am; like Sly and the Family Stone says "I Want to Thank You for Letting Me Be Myself," because I know who I am.

LIVE
(Author Unknown)

Every morning I give thanks for another day. I also look for a sign or something that I never noticed before but was right in front of me. This morning I was visiting Michigan and I sat down to drink a cup of coffee when I read the following:

LIVE your dream

Show COMPASSION

CREATE your own happiness

Follow your HEART

ENJOY the little things

LAUGH out loud

Be your BEST self

CHERISH every moment

DREAM big

EMBRACE every possibility

DISCOVER your passion

BELIEVE in miracles

CREATE peace

Make a WISH

Be SPONTANEOUS

REMEMBER to breathe

SING in the rain

Fall in LOVE

TODAY is the day

Now how did I miss reading this when it literally hang on a wall where I drink coffee every morning? We often miss encouraging words that are right in front of us daily.

IT DON'T TAKE ALL THAT, BUT IT DOES

I love to sit in the background and watch people. While I am watching I have these conversations with God. Yes conversations in that I ask "How God?" and He answers "Look." When I say "I don't understand Lord," and He says "stand still and listen." I have this great curiosity about spiritual things and how they play out in our everyday life. My conversations with God have only been going on for most of my life but they really grew when I professed Jesus Christ as my Lord and Savior and accepted my forgiveness of sin by the blood He shed for me on the cross. I just celebrated Resurrection Sunday as did many who are reading right now. I had an eye-opening experience and my life has opened up in new and exciting ways. Let me encourage you by saying that being a Christian is not boring first of all and it is exciting in so many ways to watch a life transformed. I really want to share briefly some of the things I notice as I sit in the background.

My first observation is of the men and women called to serve from the pulpit. When one is actually called to serve in the church as the mouth piece for God, it requires a transformation that if others knew what was required to accept this calling they would quickly run the other way. Think for just a moment what is required; thankfully He who calls also equips. Just in one week, there is a death in a family and a home-going has to be planned and preached, one of the sisters had a surgery and there has to be a hospital visit, the young couple who got married three months ago wants counsel, preparing bible study lesson, need word from God for Sunday sermon, meeting with leaders of the church and this is just those things related to ministry. Forget not the fact that this same one, who has been called and is also equipped by God, also has a family and life outside of the church building and wears many hats there as well. They have the same family issues that everyone else deals with and balancing all of these relationships requires one to rely on God. The decisions which they have to make are not always received by all but when these decisions are God centered they will not fail. Study and preparation has to take place and preaching and teaching without preparation no longer serves to just give people a real good feeling yet walk away with the same unchanged issue they had when they walked in the door. I sit in the background and watch the one who is called pour out wisdom from God and the problem is not lack of preparation but lack of God's children to take it and apply it to our life so we can walk in the new transformed life God desires us to live. Now next week the one who is called preaches and teaches once again to people who have never applied the last teaching to their life and thus there is no visible change but he/she must keep pouring out even if there is only one who gets it.

I sometimes think that this one who is called and is truly in love with our God and God's people may feel unappreciated sometimes and this is why I am writing this message. God sees and knows your heart and there are people out in the pews that see and know your heart as well. You are not placed on a pedestal but you are placed on your knees interceding for people. In order to deliver message that can change a life if the one who hears it applies it, you have to have time with God and study deeper than the average bible reading person. Ultimately it is God who gives the revelation of His words to us all. I would want to say to this one who is called by God that others pray for you behind the scenes and actually watch and understand a portion of what you experience in your life. I would only want to encourage you by saying it is not done in vain and your reward is great in heaven but also here on earth. Believe me everyone who was called did not answer and everyone who was called did not stand under the pressure that was on them from the very people they were called to serve. Those of you who are still standing in spite of, I thank God for you. I will say it again, I thank God for you. It is not in vain.

My second observation is of the men and women who are raising children in a world that is so very different than it was during the time I raised my children. It is truly different from the times my parents raised me. Stands to reason why we should hold onto most of what that was like and yet change the way we think and deal with what it is right now. What would my mother say if she saw some of the commercial ads on television now? The language and the shows that is now everyday entertainment would make her eyebrow go up. My hat is off to all the mothers, fathers, and partners, sisters, brothers, aunties and uncles, foster and adopted families who have the awesome responsibility of helping to develop young minds and lives in the world we live in today. Teaching young people the difference between right and wrong, good and bad, compassion and selfishness, giving and saving, respect and disrespect; these teachings and many more remain the same teachings we were taught in the past. The problem becomes teaching how to avoid the many pitfalls that can land our children in bad places. There are so many ways that evil and danger can ease into their life. I have great admiration for parents today, those who are single or married with this assignment to nurture young lives. The most recent years have been most difficult for families and parents need to know they are not alone and if they need help please ask for it. Our children are a lot smarter than we sometimes give them credit for and they have more ways to get and understand information than we did at their age. I thank God for you all. I will say it again, thank you. It is not in vain and you are also appreciated.

My third observation is of others who serve in the church as Leaders. I thank you for your service and pray you look to God who has equipped you for your reward rather than those who you serve in the various congregations. There is a grave necessity for balance in your life. Enjoy your life outside of your assigned church duties. Believe me your family will be thankful. God desires that you are good stewards over all things in your life.

It goes without saying that as a person, who sits in the background and watches people, I have many more observations but I will save them for another time. For all those who say it don't take all that, I simply say sometimes it does. If you are not walking in those shoes then you may feel it does not; but for me who watches people interact, I can say sometimes it really does.

YOU CAN'T FOOL ME, I KNOW LOVE

You can't fool me, I know love

I waited for you to come but three hours later you were a NO SHOW

I tried to call you and you would not answer the cell phone

You can't fool me, I know love

Things went wrong on your job today and they wrote you up

Now you are home and I am the one you yell at and then slap

You can't fool me, I know love

You forgot my birthday, our anniversary and Valentine's Day is just another day to you

You can't fool me, I know love

You call me stupid, to fat or to thin, you tear me down with your mouth

Don't you know that verbal abused is just as painful as physical abuse?

You can't fool me, I know love

What you do or don't do as the man of the house will prove to be an example of how

A man should treat a woman to your son and yes to your daughter

You can't fool me I know love, and this IS NOT IT

I stayed home today with a bad cold and you called to check on me three times

You finished work and came home to prepared dinner for the children and soup for me

You can't fool me, I know love

I found a single rose in the seat of my car this morning as I left home for work

There were flowers on my desk when I got there for no special reason

You can't fool me, I know love

My father became very ill and could no longer live alone

It was you who before I could ask what are we going to do now, that re-arranged the

room downstairs to accommodate his hospital bed

You can't fool me, I know love

I had a bad day at work and everything that could go wrong did; I just wanted to talk about it even though I know you can't fix it and you not only listened you heard me

You can't fool me, I know love

When I get totally overwhelmed with life until I am in tears, you get up from looking at

your sports and just hug me and then just hold me, and place my head on your shoulder

You can't fool me, I know love and this IS IT

Remember love is not shown through physical or verbal abuse. Love does not leave you

waiting and alone; it always says "Don't worry, I got you." It is supportive, encouraging

always there for you when you need it. It puts you first and makes you feel like the

Queen you are. Love shows up every day without fail and will chase you down if you

ignore it.

You can't fool me, I know love

CONCLUSION—Tenacity—Strength of Purpose—Be Tenacious

copyright © 2011

Phyllis L. Jones

CONCLUSION

Tenacity—Strength of Purpose—Be Tenacious

My desire is that you have read these pages and will pursue your dreams and passions no matter what obstacles may stand in your way. Don't give up just seek another way to accomplish your goal. If you find that it is the wrong time, then wait and try again and again. Remember that sometimes the harder the way the bigger the pay. In other words the harder it is to get there, the bigger the reward once you do.

Other may not see you as an author, a lawyer, a doctor, a teacher, a nurse or a successful business entrepreneur but you have to see yourself as one. Always listen to the story you tell yourself in your own mind because "as a man thinks so is he." This is true and I would add to that statement, "out of the heart the mouth speaks." Your words will always call into existence whatever you believe in your heart about yourself. See yourself as what you want to be. At the risk of others thinking you are crazy, speak and act as if it already is a reality. Remember that faith is also an action word; "faith without works is dead."

When you arrive, don't forget the journey. Give thanks to God for the trip and the tenacious spirit and strength to finish the course. If everything came easy you would not appreciate all the work it took to get to your goal. It may be that you are called to go a different path than others before you and whatever you do remember God cannot be put into a box, nether can your dreams. Those dreams are a gift

---

from God waiting for you to choose to open them and live your life to its fullest while you are here.

Please use the following page to get a view of where you are right now in the pursuit of the dream and what you need to do next to accomplish it. "Write the vision make it clear."

Tenacity To Do It Anyway

What is my dream/passion?

_____

_____

_____

_____

_____

_____

What story am I telling myself?

_____

_____

_____

_____

_____

Do I believe by faith it will happen?

_____

_____

_____

_____

_____

What are my short and long term goals?

_____

_____

_____

_____

_____

_____

What is my projected time to accomplish my goal?

_____

_____

_____

_____

_____

_____

I would like to hear from you as you move towards your dreams. You can reach me at **The Tenacity To Do It Anyway** on Facebook, please be my friend. I am also available by email at (tenacity2doit@ gmail.com) and there will be additional information on my upcoming books at www.PhyllisLJones.com I look forward to hearing from you and sharing if something in the pages you have read has inspired you to be tenacious. Don't give up.